WITHDRAWN

D1400513

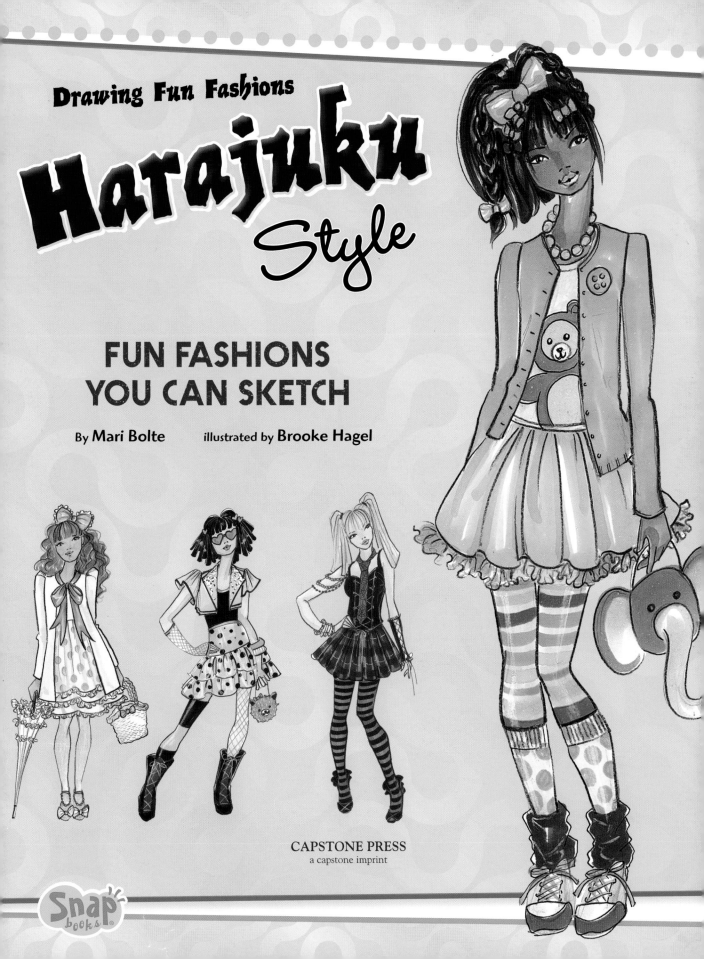

Drawing Fun Fashions

Harajuku Style

FUN FASHIONS YOU CAN SKETCH

By **Mari Bolte**   illustrated by **Brooke Hagel**

CAPSTONE PRESS
a capstone imprint

Snap books

Table of Contents

Getting Started

The Harajuku district is a short stretch of road in Tokyo. After World War II (1939–1945), curious Japanese people would visit the area. They wanted to see the clothing worn by the families of American soldiers stationed there.

As Japan's economy rose, so did its fashion scene. Teens flocked to Harajuku to see the latest fashions from stylists who were now based there.

In the late 1990s, photographer Shoichi Aoki noticed a new trend. Teens were pairing traditional Japanese clothing with designer pieces and secondhand or homemade items. He began photographing these styles. In 1997 he launched the magazine *FRUiTS* to show off those photos.

Each outfit shows step-by-step instructions on how to draw your very own fashion model. Build upon simple shapes, and use erasable guidelines to create a human shape.

TIP: Harajuku is the perfect subject to experiment with colors, textures, and hairstyles.

STEP 1: Start with a simple line drawing. Pick your favorite pose, and use light guidelines to build your model.

STEP 2: Darken the outlines, and start adding in details like hemlines and hand placements.

STEP 3: Erase guidelines, and draw in things like fabric prints, hair, facial features, and accessories.

STEP 4: Finish any final details and then add in color, textures, and shading to bring your model to life.

TIP: Although outfits appear to be a mishmash of styles, Harajuku dressers are careful in what they wear. Outfits and accessories should flow together—or make a statement by not matching.

CUTE KAWAII

In Japanese, "kawaii" means "pretty" or "cute." This fashion style has a sweet, feminine look without being too girly. A ruffled skirt is set off with belts and bows that give this outfit layers of detail.

TIP: Harajuku style is about layers of clothing working together. Make sure each piece works with the others.

Gothic Girl

Gothic fashion gained fame in America in the late 1990s after celebs were seen sporting black outfits. But Gothic style in Japan was already famous, and is much different. Girlishness and innocence are themes Japanese Goths like to feature.

TIP: Don't get distracted by dark colors. Goth girls are cute and confident!

CYBERPUNK Show-off

Cyberpunk style was first featured in *FRUiTS* magazine in the late 1990s. This style, which combines technology and Gothic fashion, makes the space age look sweet.

TIP: Bright colors, wild prints, and unusual materials bring out the sci-fi side of Harajuku.

9

Baby, You're Sweet

Frills, lace, and bows are part of the most well-known Harajuku style, known as Loli. A modernized take on elegant, vintage clothing, Loli style brings antique dolls to life.

TIP: Use dark colors instead of light to turn this into a Goth-Loli look.

VISUAL-KEI

Japanese rock bands began adopting the popular Goth-Loli look. Then they incorporated their wardrobes into their music. This style-to-song crossover is called visual-kei.

TIP: In Japanese, visual-kei translates to "visual music style." Extreme makeup and costumes match the dark, creepy music they pair with.

Decora'd Out

Short for "decoration," decora is the most colorful Harajuku style. A rainbow of hues, hair clips, and lots of layers make decora dressers stand out in a crowd.

TIP: Decora is a great style to practice using a variety of colors and tones. Try using a combination of colored pencils, markers, and crayons.

Elegant Loli

Emphasize the Goth half of Goth-Loli with serious colors and romantic ruffles. Ribbons, bows, frills, curls, and lace make a dark, Gothic outfit soft and flirty.

TIP: The layers and frills of this outfit are perfect for practicing shading techniques.

MIXED TRADITIONS

The origin of Harajuku style was the combination of traditional Japanese clothing with Western style. Some call this style wamono. Kimonos are updated with American-style fabrics and prints. Modern accessories finish the crossover between past and present.

TIP: Go crazy with prints!
Animal prints, plaids, polka
dots, ginghams, and floral
patterns will set off this
original outfit.

URA-HARA

"Ura" means "under" in Japanese. The name Ura-Hara signifies the reserved, underground aspect of this Harajuku style. Ura-Hara is a combination of hip-hop, graffiti, and skater trends. It is Harajuku's take on male fashion.

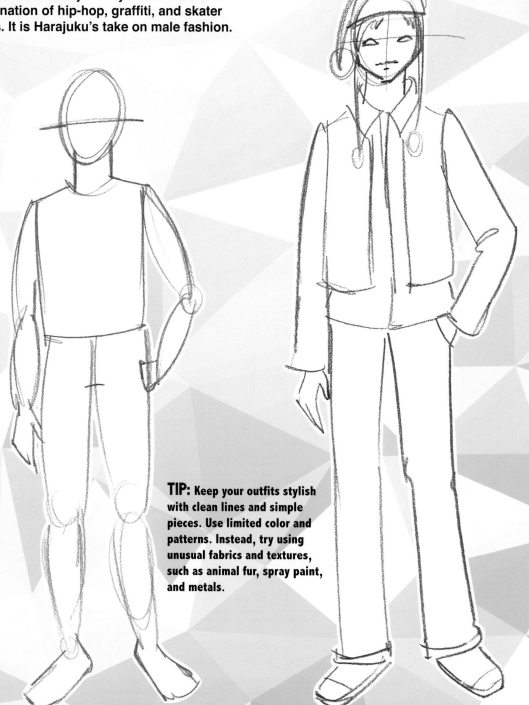

TIP: Keep your outfits stylish with clean lines and simple pieces. Use limited color and patterns. Instead, try using unusual fabrics and textures, such as animal fur, spray paint, and metals.

21

TOKYO PUNK

Punk is an instantly-recognizable style around the world. Harajuku punk is no exception. Make a statement with dark prints, metals, zippers, and lots of layers.

TIP: Use this outfit to be fun and playful. Experiment with mixed prints and unusual layers. Punk style is about finding your own creativity.

23

Sweet as a Loli-pop

Pair the lovely look of Loli with bubblegum pink decora. Combining the two styles creates the cutest kawaii outfit ever! There's no such thing as too much pink when you're sweet as a Loli-pop.

TIP: This outfit will test your creativity! How many accessory pieces can you add before you can't think of any more?

TAKE IT TO THE STREET

A true Harajuku wearer is comfortable standing out in a crowd. Take it to the street by combining punk, kawaii, decora, and visual-kei styles. You'll be stepping out in a one-of-a-kind outfit.

TIP: Experiment with a small combination of colors to find complementary groupings. Try blue, teal, black, and white, or red, purple, white, and yellow.

27

Cosplay

Dressing up as a favorite musician or pop culture icon is called cosplay (shortened from "costume play.") Many cosplayers design and create their own costumes.

Cosplay is a huge part of Harajuku culture. Cosplayers travel to the district to show off their outfits alongside other Harajuku styles.

Anime conventions around the world are more formal places for cosplayers to get together and exchange fashion tips.

Anime, manga, and video game characters are popular cosplay choices. Japanese musicians, especially visual-kei musicians, are also top picks.

TIP: Do your research! The best cosplayers are their character's biggest fans.

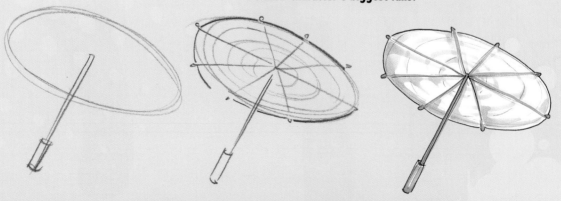

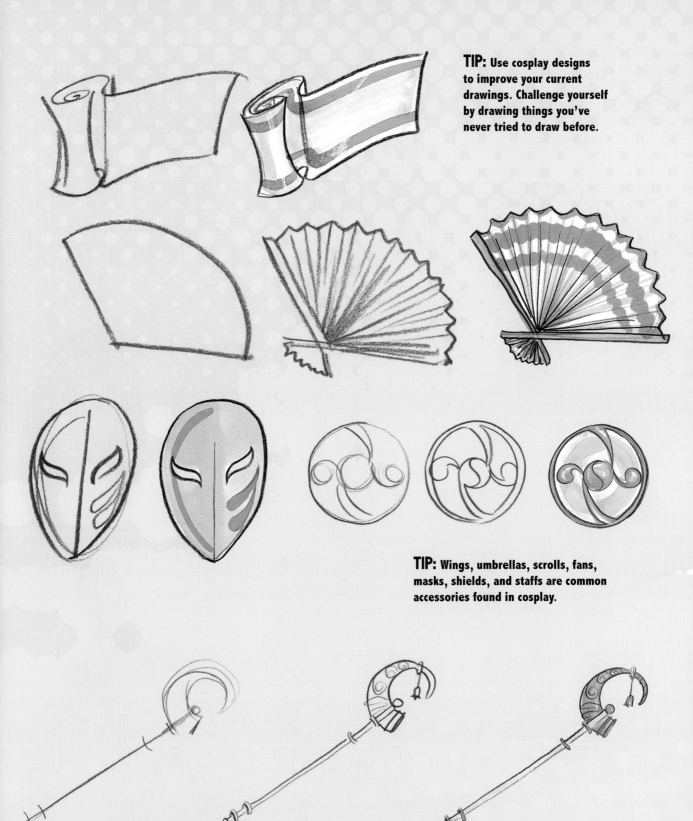

TIP: Use cosplay designs to improve your current drawings. Challenge yourself by drawing things you've never tried to draw before.

TIP: Wings, umbrellas, scrolls, fans, masks, shields, and staffs are common accessories found in cosplay.

CosPlay

TIP: School uniforms, cowl necks, bandages, and capes make regular appearances in cosplay. Spiky hair and animal ears are also common features!

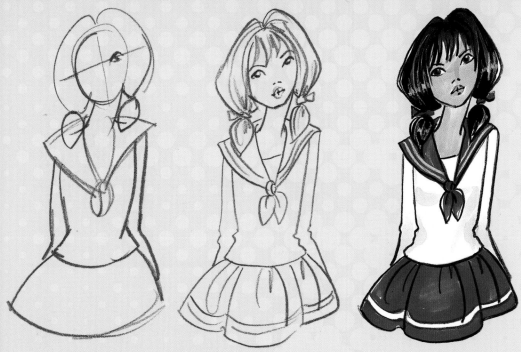

TIP: Getting the accessories right is important when cosplaying. Cosplayers spend hours making sure their costumes are as accurate as possible.

Read More

Guillain, Charlotte. *Punk: Music, Fashion, Attitude!* Culture in Action. Chicago: Raintree, 2011.

Southgate, Anna, and Keith Sparrow. *Drawing Manga Girls.* Manga Magic. New York: Rosen Central, 2012.

Torres, Laura. *Rock your Wardrobe.* QEB Rock Your ... Irvine, Calif.: QEB Pub., 2010.

Internet Sites

FactHound offers a safe, fun way to find Internet sites related to this book. All of the sites on FactHound have been researched by our staff.

Here's all you do:

Visit *www.facthound.com*

Type in this code: 9781620650349

Super-cool stuff! Check out projects, games and lots more at **www.capstonekids.com**

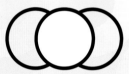

Snap Books are published by Capstone Press,
1710 Roe Crest Drive, North Mankato, Minnesota 56003
www.capstonepub.com

Copyright © 2013 by Capstone Press, a Capstone imprint. All rights reserved. No part of this publication may be reproduced in whole or in part, or stored in a retrieval system, or transmitted in any formor by any means, electronic, mechanical, photocopying, recording, or otherwise, without written permission of the publisher.

Library of Congress Cataloging-in-Publication Data
Bolte, Mari.
  Harajuku style : fun fashions you can sketch / by Mari Bolte.
    pages cm — (Snap. Drawing fun fashions)
  Summary: "Lively text and fun illustrations describe how to draw cool fashions"—Provided by publisher.
  ISBN 978-1-62065-034-9 (library binding)
  ISBN 978-1-4765-1775-9 (ebook PDF)
1. Fashion drawing—Juvenile literature. 2. Teenage girls—Clothing—Japan—Tokyo—Juvenile literature.
3. Subculture—Japan—Tokyo—Juvenile literature. I. Title.
  TT509.B6527 2013

  746.9'20835—dc23

Editorial Credits
Lori Bye, designer; Nathan Gassman, art director; Marcie Spence, media researcher;
Laura Manthe, production specialist

The illustrations in this book were created with marker and pencil.
Design elements by Shutterstock.

Printed in the United States of America in North Mankato, Minnesota.
092012   006933CGS13